Be Ye Ready

Imperatives for Being Ready for Christ

Be Ye Ready
Imperatives for Being Ready for Christ

Lance Lambert

LANCE LAMBERT MINISTRIES

Richmond, Virginia, USA

Copyright © 2016
Lance Lambert Ministries
Richmond, VA
USA
All rights reserved

ISBN: 978-1-68389-026-3
www.lancelambert.org

Unless otherwise indicated, Scripture quotations are from the American Standard Version 1901

Contents

Preface 9
1. Ready for the Coming of Christ 11
2. Imperatives for Being Ready for Christ 37

Preface

In June 2006, Lance Lambert gave a series of spoken messages at the Christian Family Conference in Richmond, Virginia. The theme of the conference was: "Summing Up All Things in Christ." As his part of the ministry, Lance shared on "Being Ready for Christ's Coming." This booklet is the transcription of that ministry with only minimal editing for clarity. It is being printed with the prayer that it can be used to help the Lord's people to prepare for His soon return.

In 1 Chronicles 12:32 the Bible says of the sons of Issachar that they were "... men who had understanding of the times, to know what Israel ought to do." May the Lord have a people today who understand the days in which we are living and are being prepared to meet the Bridegroom—the Lord Jesus.

1.
Ready for the Coming of Christ

Ephesians 1:9–10

Making known unto us the mystery of his will, according to his good pleasure which he purposed in him unto a dispensation of the fullness of the times, to sum up all things in Christ, the things in the heavens, and the things upon the earth; in him, I say.

Matthew 24:36–44

But of that day and hour knoweth no one, not even the angels of heaven, neither the Son, but the Father only. And as were the days of Noah, so shall be the coming of the Son of man. For as in those days which were before the flood they were eating and drinking, marrying and giving in marriage, until the day that Noah entered into the ark, and they knew not until the flood came, and took them all away; so shall be the coming of the Son of man. Then shall two men be in the field; one is taken, and one is left: two women shall be grinding at the mill; one is taken, and one is left. Watch therefore: for ye know not on what day your Lord cometh. But know this, that if the master of the house had known in what watch the thief was coming, he would have watched, and would not have suffered his house to be broken through. Therefore be ye also ready; for in an hour that ye think not the Son of man cometh.

Luke 12:35–40

Let your loins be girded about, and your lamps burning; and be ye yourselves like unto men looking for their lord, when he shall return from the marriage feast; that, when he cometh and knocketh, they may straightway open unto him. Blessed are those servants, whom the lord when he cometh shall find watching: verily I say unto you, that he shall gird himself, and make them sit down to meat, and shall come and serve them. And if he shall come in the second watch, and if in the third, and find them so, blessed are those servants. But know this, that if the master of the house had known in what hour the thief was coming, he would have watched, and not have left his house to be broken through. Be ye also ready: for in an hour that ye think not the Son of man cometh.

II Peter 3:10–13

But the day of the Lord will come as a thief; in the which the heavens shall pass away with a great noise, and the elements shall be dissolved with fervent heat, and the earth and the works that are therein shall be burned up. Seeing that these things are thus all to be dissolved, what manner of persons ought ye to be in all holy living and godliness, looking for and earnestly desiring the coming of the day of God, by reason of which the heavens being on fire shall be dissolved, *and the elements shall melt with fervent heat? But, according to his promise, we look for new heavens and a new earth, wherein dwelleth righteousness.*

Shall we pray?

Beloved Lord, we want to thank You for Your presence. We are not asking You to join us; we are here to be with You. And we want to thank You, Lord, that when it comes to the ministry of Your word, in the most wonderful manner, You make provision for us. You have provided us with an anointing through the finished work of our Lord Jesus, and the Holy Spirit is here to make it a reality. Lord, by faith we stand into that anointing grace and power for the speaking of Your word, for the translating of it, and for the hearing of it. Lord, touch our hearts. Do something in us. We are very conscious that we are standing together at a point in history that is significant. We want to be wholly with You in these days. Therefore, beloved Lord, we commit our time to You. Fill it with Yourself and somehow reach our hearts. Where we need to be woken up, wake us up. Where we need to be challenged, challenge us. Where we need to be equipped, equip us. Lord, make us ready in these days in which we live for Your coming. We ask it in the name of our Lord Jesus. Amen.

The Lord is Coming

This word ready is a very interesting word. It comes from a very old Greek noun that was not used even in classical Greek because it was so old. But it means "fitness," "to be ready," "to be fit," "to be prepared." It is a tremendous thought that every child of God should seriously consider because we are living in momentous days. You parents need to deeply consider this matter of being ready. You who are business men ought to be ready. All of us who are members of the body of Christ need to be ready; not just in our heads but equipped and fit for the coming of the Lord. This matter is of tremendous importance.

We will consider this matter of the coming of the Lord and being ready for Him. I want to share especially on the emphasis of our Lord Jesus whenever He spoke about His return. This point we have reached in history is amazing. I can imagine that many of those saints I knew when I was first saved many years ago would be amazed at what is happening to this world and the quickness with which things are changing all around us. You can hardly call Western nations Christian; they are essentially pagan. They have rejected the word of God and the Law of God which made them great, and made them, as it were, to be instrumental in bringing the light of the gospel to so many nations. However, you will go a long, long way today in any Western country to find vestiges of the gospel. It is gone—socially, morally, educationally, politically. Where is the church?

Not long ago a Danish newspaper published a cartoon of Mohammed and the whole Islamic world went up in smoke. Denmark and Norway lost millions and millions of dollars in business. But these countries in which you and I have been brought up in are seeing every kind of blasphemy coming in. Jerry Springer's thing in Britain, as well as the Da Vinci Code, are absolute blasphemy. There is a demonic dimension in these things which means that any child of God who goes to look at them can be influenced by these spirits. That is where we need to wake up.

How are we to be ready for the coming of the Lord? Nobody has said a thing about the Da Vinci Code. Can you believe that they are saying that Jesus married Mary Magdalene and had children which, of course, we know is fictional. But the whole Islamic world went up in smoke over a cartoon or two about Mohammed, and nobody in the Islamic world believes that Mohammed is God in the flesh. They believe he is just a prophet. But there has not been a protest from us who are supposed to be Christians, from the moderator of the church of Scotland, nor from the Archbishop of Canterbury, plus a whole number of others. It is unbelievable to me that such things can happen. Only the Pope, God bless him, has spoken up. It is unbelievable! We have reached a point in history—and passed it—and are now on the way down, and the sooner believers wake up the better.

Many Christians criticize the Charismatics, but the fact remains that whatever faults it has, it is going to go down in history as the greatest single movement of the Spirit of God since Pentecost. It has swept countless millions into the kingdom of God. It began in the sixties and it is interesting that the statistics show it has gone right through the seventies to where we are now. I hear many people putting down the Charismatics, saying they are emotional and hysterical; but I believe something tremendous happened. There was a breaching of a blockade that the enemy had made on the question of the body of Christ. No one even thought about the body of Christ, but something happened in the

Charismatic movement that made people talk about the body of Christ, the house of God, and being living stones. I know there is empire building in the whole thing, there is a whole lot that is just absolutely fraudulent, and it is dying like every other movement of the Spirit of God in the history of the church, but the fact still remains that the Lord is at work. But where are the believers who are alive, who are hearing the Lord, and who are aware of where we stand. Thus this matter of being ready for Christ is of tremendous importance.

Do you believe the Lord is coming? I do. I believe He could come now. Personally, I have certain things I believe that must take place before He comes, but I might be wrong. I would not be the least bit surprised if I heard the heavenly trumpet, that great blast on the shofar (a ram's horn), and that great shout of the Lord Jesus Himself. He is seated at the right hand of God, but He will rise to His feet and descend from heaven with a shout. Oh, what a tremendous thing it will be to hear that shout of our Lord Jesus! It will again be like "Finished!" Or "It is done!" And the voice of the archangel—I wonder what that will be: "Behold He comes as a thief!" (See Revelation 3:3.)

In a single moment of time, in the twinkling of an eye it will happen. Because the Lord has been so slow about coming you may think it is going to take a long time, that He will take days and days circling around the earth in the clouds. No, no; it says in the twinkling of an eye. Have you ever seen the twinkling of an eye? In one moment it is gone. And the dead in Christ will be raised, and we who are alive will be taken up and put on incorruption. I look forward to it so much. How amazing it will be, all done in a moment. It will be the manifestation of the summing up of everything in Christ. It is in the process now, but when He actually comes, it will be the manifestation of it. And everything that cannot be summed up in Him is closed; it is gone. It belongs to the past and will not be referred to again.

I Make All Things New

I love the way the Lord says in Revelation: "Behold, I make all things new" (21:5b). What a wonderful word! There will be no more death, no more mourning, no more crying, no more pain, no more corruption; it will all be gone. It belonged to the first things—in the parenthesis of sin—and the final bracket has been added. It is over! In a moment of time it will happen, and every true believer will be there. You say, "No, no, I am not sure about that." I am. I am absolutely sure about it. And the dead will be there because they are not dead. So if you think you are right at the point of going and you think you will not be there to see the Lord come, you will see Him. You will be the first to see Him; then we which are alive and remain will be caught up to be with the Lord forever (see 1 Thessalonians 5:16–17).

"I make all things new." It all began at Calvary. A new man, a new covenant, a new life, a new beginning all began at Calvary. The more I think about it the more excited I become because everything is new—a new heaven and a new earth wherein dwells righteousness. Sin did something to this old heaven and earth so that within it there is a corruption, a physical corruption, let alone a moral corruption. It is within the very fabric of the universe.

I think it is tremendous that there will be a new heaven and a new earth wherein dwells righteousness.

Therefore, if you are a child of God and you are born of the Spirit of God, you are a part of the new man even though you may look Caucasian, or Chinese, or you may be black or white or yellow or a tinge of red. It does not make any difference. If you are born of God you are in the new man—Jew or Gentile, one new man in Christ.

The New Jerusalem

Think of the New Jerusalem coming down out of heaven having the glory of God. All this is going to happen in a moment. Is it any wonder that the Lord descends with the shout of triumph: "It is over! It is done! The thing is completed! The whole old order has passed away, and everything is summed up in Christ."

You might think I am saying these things because I am getting old, and as we get older we think more about the coming of the Lord. I must say it will be so nice to have a new body with no aches or pains, which will cover our agility, our flexibility, and our versatility. And I rather fancy having a body that goes through walls. They all talk about taking trips to Mars or to the moon that you can book now for so many million dollars, but who wants to go in one of those things with all that gear. I had rather wait for the Lord. We will get there in a flash if it is right for us to go to such places. There is no doubt about my wishing the Lord would come quickly, but it has nothing to do with my age. I am convinced that we are in the last phase of world history, and there are a number of things that convince me.

Daniel's Prophetic Word

God gave Daniel a tremendous revelation that went all the way down through history which is called the times of the Gentiles. It was made up of Babylon, Persia, the Greeks, the Hellenistics, the Romans, and in the end something happens which is a conglomeration of them all so that both in the first coming of the Lord and the last coming of the Lord, this incredible empire will be back in its place. If I understand Revelation 13, 14, 15, it is a final restoration of this whole terrible thing that was the attempts of the enemy to take the world.

I am often asked why the Chinese are not in the Old Testament. Simene is in the Old Testament and that means in Hebrew "China or the Chinese people." It is there, but all the great empires that were not attempts by Satan to take the world are not mentioned. It is only those that were demonically inspired. Therefore we have Babylon, Persia, Hellenism, and Romanism—four great empires. Why am I so sure that the Lord is coming in my lifetime? Why am I so sure that we are in the last phase of world history however long it lasts? There are certain things that have been fulfilled that have never been fulfilled before.

The Lord said to Daniel: "Shut up the book and seal it, Daniel, until the time of the end. And then the Lord gives two little clues: "Many shall run to and fro in the earth, and knowledge shall be increased" (see 12:4). Every time I sit in the London airport or Kennedy or Washington or Atlanta, or any other airport and see people going back and forward, rushing here and rushing there, trains carrying people here and there, people queuing up here and there, and I think, "many shall run to and fro." Isn't it amazing that you can get anywhere in the world now within twenty hours!

"And knowledge shall increase." Have you ever thought about the internet? I am computer illiterate, but I am amazed at the expansion of knowledge there is through the internet all over the world. Something colossal is happening that even Maoism could not stop, Communism could not stop, and Islam cannot stop it. It is something that has burst through every border and no one can do anything about it.

"Shut up the book until the time of the end. Many shall run to and fro." Has there ever been a time in the whole history of the world when men and women have literally covered the globe within hours? And I am not talking about a hundred; I am talking about thousands, millions in the end. Has there ever been a time when knowledge has been so increased and so available? I would say we have to be somewhere in the last phase, in the very things that God showed to Daniel, and the consummation of it all. And we hear those wonderful words about the One who shall come near to the Ancient of days and shall receive a kingdom that is eternal.

The Recreation of the Jewish State

Then I think of little Israel. On the 14th of May, 1948 one of the most amazing cataclysmic events took place in the history of the whole world. It has never taken place before, not in all the chronicles and annals of world history. A nation that was scattered for one thousand eight hundred years came back to its homeland against all odds. I am not talking about the political rights and wrongs.

I am talking about the fact that on the 14th of May the Jewish state was recreated within its homeland in the Middle East, amazingly within the Islamic homeland. Can you believe such a thing could have happened! How could it have happened? It is a miracle. Nobody can tell me this is a coincidence. One great evangelical said: "It is a political coincidence, accident, a coincidence of history." Some accident! Some coincidence! That is all I can say.

Twice the Jewish people have been exiled from their homeland and twice they have been returned to it. The first time was seventy years in captivity a thousand miles east. The second time was when they were scattered one thousand nine hundred years to the far north, far east, far south, far west, and then brought back. However, it was not when the Jewish people were the strongest but when two-thirds of our people died in the most horrific circumstances in the Nazi holocaust. And when Israel was the weakest, the most heart-broken, and it seemed the most impossible, the miracle happened, and Israel reappeared on the world scene exactly as the prophet said it would, and exactly as the Lord Jesus said: "Learn the parable of the fig tree."

On the 7th of June, 1967 another cataclysmic event took place and a large part of the church of God was asleep. Jerusalem came back in its entirety to the Jewish people. The Lord Jesus said: "And Jerusalem shall be trodden down under the feet of the Gentiles [the non-Jews] until the times of the Gentiles be fulfilled." Never before since Pentecost has there been anything like this! That means we have to be in the last phase of world history.

This is not just something to do with Jewish business men, Jewish tycoons, or people pulling strings behind the scenes.

It is nonsense. These people were a broken-hearted people, survivors of the most terrible genocide in history. They had nowhere to go. Do you know that there were some two million children orphaned without anywhere to go? Do you know that many of those who went back to their homes in Poland and Lithuania were murdered? The father and brother of Shamir (one of our prime ministers) were murdered by Polish neighbors when they went back to find their home. There is no record in history like this.

What does God say? Through the prophet Jeremiah God said this: "Hear the word of the Lord, O ye nations, and declare it in the isles afar off; and say, He that scattered Israel will gather him, and keep him, as a shepherd doth his flock" (Jeremiah 31:10). He is not speaking to the Jewish people. He said, "Hear the word of the Lord, O ye nations, declare it in the isles that are afar off," as if God is saying, "This is a sign of the coming end. This is a sign of the consummation of the age. I scattered this people and I have gathered them, and I have kept them as a shepherd does his flock." That in itself is extraordinary. In fifty-seven years since 1948 there have been seven wars, four of which should have been the liquidation of Israel, and in every one of them she has triumphed. It is a shepherd keeping his flock. But someone says, "I do not know why you are talking like this. All these things were fulfilled years ago in the return from Babylon." Really? Do you know your Bible?

The Lord says, "I have loved you with an everlasting love: therefore with lovingkindness have I drawn you. Again shall you plant vineyards upon the mountains of Samaria. You shall plant the vines and you shall enjoy the fruit thereof" (see Jeremiah

31:3–5). There you have a time frame. When they returned from the exile in Babylon, they never re-colonized Samaria. They found it a hotchpotch of mongrel peoples, and they would not touch them. Nehemiah would not allow them to take part in the rebuilding of the walls of Jerusalem. Ezra chased them out of the temple. They would have nothing to do with these Samaritans. And you know the story in the New Testament in John 4 when Jesus sat by the well and actually said to the woman: "Give Me to drink," and she said, "What, You a Jew, a rabbi asking water of me, a Samaritan woman? Don't You know that Jews and Samaritans have nothing whatsoever to do with each other?" So even in the New Testament they never re-colonized Samaria. That means there is a time frame for this amazing word of the Lord: "Hear the word of the Lord, O ye nations and declare it in the isles that are afar off; He that scattered Israel will gather him and keep him as a shepherd does his flock."

The Time Frame
What is the time frame? It is something to do with Samaria. In 1968 Jewish settlers began to plant vineyards upon the mountains of Samaria, and this is a fulfillment of God's word. Now there are those who want to give it all away, but it does not matter. The fact is you have the time frame. Now we know that when the Lord said this: "Hear the word of the Lord O ye nations; declare it in the isles afar off: he that scattered Israel will gather him," it is something to do with our day and generation. It means that the coming of the Lord is near. Thank God!

When I see the wickedness and the pollution that are in this world, all that we have done to this world, which was a charge from God that we would keep it, we have failed; we have not kept it. We have not only exploited it but we have destroyed it. I know Christians are not very interested in environmental things and feel somehow or other that the whole thing is a big scam. But God made a solemn charge to Adam and Eve: "You are to keep this earth, till it, guard it, and you are to multiply;" and we have failed. This world cannot go on much longer. When He comes, how will He deal with the corruption that is in the world physically? What will happen to animals when they do not die in the same way? It is all in Romans 8 and has to do with the gospel. It is a redemption, not only to do with us but with the whole world—feather, fur, and fin. What a redemption! It means that any child of God who is asleep is crazy. I think any Christian who is asleep in this day and generation is stupid, and if we are swept away by the events that will suddenly come upon us like a tsunami, we cannot blame the Lord. You and I have had every evidence given to us of the point in history that we have come to. We need to be awake.

There are many things one could talk about in the present juncture we have arrived at, and I will only touch on them very briefly.

Globalization

Globalization is not wrong, is it? Well, it would not be wrong if the right person were in charge. If the Lord Jesus was here with that kind of globalization, that is different. But this kind of globalization is all to do with Babel. Babel is where it began—one world, one language, one people. How interesting it is that that is the motto of the European Parliament, and they have actually built a building, according to a Dutch fifteenth century painter, of the tower of Babel. If you take Babel then you have Babylon, and when we go through the Bible we find Babylon is destroyed and it is found in the book of Revelation in chapters 14, 15, 16, 17, 18. It is Babylon, Babylon; it is all Babylon. Just remember that in Hebrew this Babylon is the Greek name for Babel. The Hebrew is Ba-bil. In our Bible they always put it as Babylon because it makes much more sense, but if you read the Hebrew Bible it is Ba-bil all the way from Genesis, chapter 11, through to the time of Nebuchadnezzar. And in the Hebrew New Testament it is Ba-bil as found in the book of Revelation.

What were they doing in Babel? They spoke one language; therefore, they did not have to have translation. They were all one people. It was the first city ever built, and in those cities there were some kind of high-rise buildings. Now because we are all so superior in the twenty-first century we naturally think of them as poor sort of creatures, so probably the buildings were only four-stories high. They could not build something like they have in Manhattan. After all they all came from tadpoles and did not have that kind of mentality. They were all hairy with brains like peas.

What was it? It is not a fairy story. It was so significant to God, so vital to God that He came down and destroyed their understanding of one another and thus put a divine brake upon the whole thing which has lasted until this century. By causing a multiplicity of languages it caused a multiplicity of cultures and groups that became ethnic groups; therefore a divine brake was put upon it which caused great limitation. What were they trying to do? Was it the first space exploration? "Ridiculous! Only the twentieth century could get a man to the moon." I am not so sure that mankind has evolved. I think he has devolved. I think Adam and the others were incredibly clever and intelligent; vastly more so than most of us today. And whatever that tower was that they were building, it was of such significance to the Lord—whether it was space exploration or as some people have believed it was occult (I do not know)—the Lord put a brake on it. Now that brake is off. We have put a man on the moon and we have a moon buggy running around on the moon. We are exploring Mars and have even gone to Venus. It is amazing. The brake is off. I believe they could have cloned a human being at that time, which would have been fallen human beings if they had been left to themselves. Now all these centuries later fallen man has for the first time cloned a sheep, a dog, and it is only a question of time before they clone a human being. Now if we start cloning human beings, will it be spirit, soul, and body? Or are they candidates for demon possession?

It is no wonder the Lord put a brake on this thing in Babel and stopped it. All the way through history there have been the attempts of Babylon, Persia, the Hellenists, and the Romans to try and somehow take the whole world but the brake has always been there until the twentieth and twenty-first centuries.

It cannot be very long before the antichrist appears, the one who will lead the whole world, becoming the darling of the world, giving it a new order and a new way of living. People always think the antichrist will be a cross between Adolph Hitler, Stalin and Nero, all three rolled into one. I do not; I think he will be much more like some of your American politicians—suave, intelligent, good-looking, falling into sin regularly and somehow or other being forgiven by the whole world. That is going to be the antichrist.

Psalm 2, which is a Messianic psalm, is a prophetic window into what is happening at present in the world. "Why do the nations imagine a vain thing? Their kings and rulers take counsel together against the Lord and against His Messiah saying, 'Let us cast away their bonds and break their fetters" (see vv. 1–3). In other words, they are going to say the Law of God, the word of God is unhealthy. It puts the human brain into a straitjacket. It is not like the beautiful humanism of Hellenism where the mind can go out and out, where everything is the product of the human mind. It began with man and ends with man. That is humanism—666—fallen man.

I find this so tremendous; therefore I find it very hard to understand why Christians do not get bowled over by these facts. Why do we not wake up? But if there is a paralysis in the Western world, thank God there is not one in the third world. Tremendous things are happening there with thousands coming to the Lord. I was in Singapore with one of the brothers that helps me, and we went past a column of young people one-mile-long—playing guitars, reading the Bible, in circles praying. They were waiting to go into one of the mega churches. I know some people say, "It is all sort of superficial, very shallow, but when I spoke with some of the leaders, they said, "We are very conscious of it, but what are we to do? We are swamped by those turning to the Lord." Isn't this amazing? I would thank God on bended knee if in Britain I saw a column one-mile-long of mid-teenagers waiting to get into a meeting to worship the Lord and hear His word. I would thank God whether it is shallow or not; it is a beginning. Thank God for it! What are these poor men to do when thousands are turning to the Lord? How are they to counsel?

The Emphasis of Our Lord on His Return

There is a total rejection of God's word, His Law, and the Lord Jesus. Our Lord gave a major discourse on His return which is recorded in Matthew's Gospel, chapters 24—25, in Mark's Gospel, chapter 13, and in Luke's Gospel, chapter 21, and we must also add chapters 12 and 17 of Luke. What was the emphasis of our Lord Jesus? People always ask me: "Do you believe we are all going to go before the tribulation? Or will we all go through the tribulation? Or will some of us be taken during the tribulation?" I have my own definite view, and upon that view I believe I cannot be budged. I believe in a partial rapture of those who are ready at the beginning of the tribulation. However, I must tell you that I do not find the Lord's emphasis on the sequence of events or even the events themselves. He speaks of the sequence of events; He speaks of the birth pangs of the coming kingdom; He speaks of the final phase—the abomination of desolation standing where it ought not to stand. He speaks of all kinds of things that are unfolding, but that is not His emphasis. His emphasis is contained in these words: "Therefore, be ye also ready for in an hour that you think not the Son of Man comes." Take heed to yourselves—take heed to your hearts, and take heed that no man leads you astray. That is His emphasis. You find it everywhere you turn. And this is the thing I find so amazing and so completely overlooked in the charts that give us every single thing worked out from beginning to end, exactly how it is going to happen, when it is going to happen, and all the rest of it. And some of the folks who get wrapped up in Biblical prophecy are the most unprepared people in this world for the coming of the Lord.

Be Alert and Watch

The new versions say, "Be alert;" "watch." We find it again and again and again. This major discourse was not given to the unsaved multitude or to the great company of followers of the Lord Jesus at that point. Nor was it given to the one hundred and twenty who were finally to be in that upper room or to the seventy who went out in His name and saw Satan falling from heaven, healing the sick, cleansing the leper—and not even to the twelve. It was given to an inner circle of the twelve—Andrew, Peter, James, and John—the most responsible of all the apostles, the inner circle of the inner circle. To these the Lord Jesus said looking into their eyes: "Watch, for you know not what day your Lord comes." Or again, "Be ye also ready for in an hour you think not the Son of Man comes." Now the Lord knew that they would not be present at that coming. He knew they were going to die and be with Him; so why did He tell them this? Did He not give it to wake us up? In other words, the most responsible of us may not be ready. Those who are the most involved in the work of the Lord, those who have the heaviest burden upon their shoulders can get lost in the work, get lost in the routine, get lost in our knowledge of Biblical prophecy and not be ready for His coming. Why did the Lord say again and again, "When you think not ..."? Did you notice the Son of Man comes when you think not? Be ye also ready.

The Ten Virgins

We find this in the parable of the ten virgins, and there are many believers for whom this comes as a terrible shock. We often hear this as a gospel address, and I thank God for every one who has gotten saved in such a gospel address. But the ten virgins were ten virgins, and nowhere in the word of God is an unsaved person, still in their sin, called a virgin. They are called adulterers and adulteresses and lots of other things but never a virgin. These were ten virgins. Secondly, they were all related to the Bridegroom. Thirdly, they all had torches. Fourthly, they all had torches alight. They were not just holding a dead torch. Fifthly, they all had oil in their torches. Wherein was the difference? The difference was in reserves. Five of them had reserved flasks with oil, emergency reserves, and five of them did not. When the wedding was delayed and they were waiting, as so often happens in our weddings in Asia, finally the Bridegroom appears, and the cry goes out: "Behold the Bridegroom!" They all go out; but the five panic and say, "He has come so late that our lamps are going out." They actually said, "Our lamps are going out." Thus we know they were still alight. This means the parable of the ten virgins is much more serious than most Christians understand. And the Lord said, "Be ready." That is how He ended that parable. I say this is of tremendous importance.

The Confusion Over His Coming

Do you not think the Lord knew the confusion there would be over this question of His coming? Do you think He was just ignorant of it and has remained ignorant of it and is just now waking up? "My word, they are very confused. Some of them believe they are going before the tribulation, some right through the tribulation at the very end, and others think only those who are ready are going to be taken and the rest purified." Do you not think our Lord would have said: "I really must give a five or ten-minute supplementary discourse and clear up this thing once and for all? I will spell it out exactly as it will be. It will not be before the tribulation and it will not be after the tribulation. It will be during the tribulation, and it will be for those who are ready." (I am giving you my understanding of it.) Then it would have been absolutely clear to all of us. Why did He not do that? I believe the ambiguity of our Lord Jesus is deliberate. He was not going to give us some kind of chart that would enable us to go so far in sin and then say, "Now I must wake up because He is definitely coming." In other words, if you want to continue in sin, you can continue, and if you want to continue in lukewarmness, you can continue in lukewarmness. And if you want to say to yourself, "People have always thought He was coming, so I do not think He is coming just yet, maybe in another generation or two." You can think that but if the Spirit of God stirs you, you can be ready for His coming. Consider for a moment: the best thing of all is to be ready; then if we are all taken before the tribulation we will be ready and not ashamed. And if we are going to go through the tribulation, we can at least be prepared and ready for what comes, and if only those who are ready are taken, then we are ready. We cannot lose if we are ready. It is so simple.

Paul's Exhortation to Watch

When you come to the three apostles—Paul, Peter, and John—every time they touched on the return of the Lord Jesus it is the same emphasis. In the first Thessalonian letter Paul said: "You know, brothers and sisters, what the seasons are. I have no need to write to you, but you need to wake up. You need to be alive; you need to wake up. Don't sleep like the rest. Don't be drunk in the night like others. We do not belong to the night; we belong to the day. Let us therefore be sober and watchful" (5:1–7).

When I was a boy, my mother was ill at one point and had to have an operation. She was taken to the hospital and an aunt came to look after my sister and me. One night my aunt burst into my bedroom, pulled the curtain aside, and said, "Lance, get up; the whole avenue is filled with police cars and dogs and policemen." I stumbled out of my bedroom across the landing into my mother's bedroom and saw my sister hanging out of the window with my aunt discussing who was being burgled. There were policemen everywhere with German shepherd dogs, flashlights and big black police cars. My aunt was saying, "I think it is so and so," and my sister said, "No, they have a huge dog in that house. The thief would not last a minute if that dog got hold of him." Then my aunt said, "I think I will go downstairs and make myself a cup of coffee." Off she went while my sister and I continued to watch all the events going on in the avenue. A few moments later we heard the most blood curdling scream that was enough to raise the dead in the cemetery across the River Thames. There was my aunt standing on the landing of the stairs shaking like a leaf, white as milk, and she said, "The thief is in our kitchen."

Then I said, "Did he say anything?"

And my aunt said, "He said, 'Good evening, madam.'"

Then my sister said, "What was he doing?"

And my aunt said, "He was eating one of the milk puddings."

He went out the way he came in through a tiny little window. They never caught him that night but one year later they caught him. He was a famous cat burglar and had broken in thirteen houses that night. Would you believe it? We had been discussing who had been burgled and he was in our kitchen. It is amazing. And I have thought to myself ever since about Christians who say, "So and so is going to get caught out by the coming of the Lord." But maybe we could be caught out by the coming of the Lord. We need to watch, be alive, and be ready.

Peter's Exhortation to Holy Living

Then I thought also of Peter in this passage in II Peter: "What manner of person ought you to be" (see 3:11). He does not give you a chart or a whole sequence of events; rather he says, "This is what is going to happen; the whole thing is going up. This world has had its baptism in water; now it is going to have its baptism in fire." Therefore he says, "What manner of person ought you to be in all holy living and godliness?" That is the emphasis—ready for Christ.

John's Exhortation to Keep Our Garment

I think of John and how he recorded this amazing word. Of course he was recording something he saw, but it was really the Lord Himself who was speaking. In Revelation 16, suddenly in the middle of this whole thing about Armageddon it says, "Behold, I come as a thief. Blessed is he that watcheth, and keepeth his garments, lest he walk naked, and they see his shame" (v. 15). Right in the midst of this whole thing about Armageddon, and there are so many ideas about Armageddon—when it is going to take place, how it is going to take place, and the rest of it—but here we have this word: "I am coming as a thief; see to it that you are not found naked."

Then we have the words of our Lord Jesus in the last chapter of the Bible: "And he saith unto me, Seal not up the words of the prophecy of this book; for the time is at hand. He that is unrighteous, let him do unrighteousness still more: and he that is filthy, let him be made filthy still: and he that is righteous, let him do righteousness still, and he that is holy, let him be made holy still. Behold, I come quickly; and my reward is with me, to render to each man according as his work is. I am the Alpha and the Omega, the first and the last, the beginning and the end. Blessed are they that wash their robes, that they may have the right to come to the tree of life, and may enter in by the gates into the city" (Revelation 22:10–15).

This is the most unevangelical word in the New Testament: "He is that is unrighteous, let him continue on and become more unrighteous." Who is the Lord speaking to? He is speaking to believers—the seven churches. He that is unrighteous, okay, continue on. He that is unholy, let him become even more unholy, and he that is righteous, let him become even more so, and he that is holy let him become more so. It is as if the Lord is saying, "If you do not want to wake up, you do not have to."

Now that is what I mean about the ambiguity of the Lord. I have no doubt in my own mind as to what is right—but the ambiguity of it. The way He speaks about this matter is almost as if He is saying, "If you want to wake up, wake up. If you want to be ready, get ready. If you want to be prepared, get prepared. If you want to be equipped, be equipped. But if you do not, go on the way you are going. This is a serious word. We all have such a deceitfulness in us when it comes to sin, like Achan we bury it in the tent. We cannot do anything with it, so we bury it in the tent. It is there; it is on our conscience. We know where it is. The Lord knows where it is, and we do not do anything about it. I think it is interesting to note the emphasis of the Lord Jesus and the emphasis of the apostles when it comes to the return of the Lord Jesus. It is all to do with watching, taking heed, being ready.

May the Lord use this word to challenge us and to enable us to wake up. We do not know how much more time we have but we can be sure that the only safe thing is to be ready. There is no insurance when it comes to the return of the Lord and what will happen other than to be ready. When we are ready, we are insured.

May the Lord use this word to touch our hearts and to wake us up to some of the things that are happening with such rapidity all around us. There has been a little respite in the States in many ways, but only a little. The fight is on to destroy the last vestiges of Biblical conscience, Biblical principles in this nation, and when that is gone, then like an Amazon flood the enemy will sweep over the western world. It is all in place with the rise of the European Union, the deterioration of the Unites States, and the huge forces at work in Asia. May the Lord touch us, challenge us, and wake us up.

2.
Imperatives for Being Ready for Christ

Ephesians 1:9–10
Making known unto us the mystery of his will, according to his good pleasure which he purposed in him unto a dispensation of the fullness of the times, to sum up all things in Christ, the things in the heavens, and the things upon the earth; in him, I say.

Matthew 24:38–44
For as in those days which were before the flood they were eating and drinking, marrying and giving in marriage, until the day that Noah entered into the ark, and they knew not until the flood came, and took them all away; so shall be the coming of the Son of man. Then shall two men be in the field; one is taken, and one is left: two women shall be grinding at the mill; one is taken, and one is left. Watch therefore; for ye know not on what day your Lord cometh. But know this, that if the master of the house had known in what watch the thief was coming, he would have watched, and would not have suffered his house to

be broken through. Therefore be ye also ready; for in an hour that ye think not the Son of man cometh.

II Peter 3:11–13
Seeing that these things are thus all to be dissolved, what manner of persons ought ye to be in all holy living and godliness, looking for and hastening the coming of the day of God, by reason of which the heavens being on fire shall be dissolved, and the elements shall melt with fervent heat? But, according to his promise, we look for new heavens and a new earth, wherein dwelleth righteousness.

Ephesians 5:15–21
Look therefore carefully how ye walk, not as unwise, but as wise; redeeming the time, because the days are evil. Wherefore be ye not foolish, but understand what the will of the Lord is. And be not drunken with wine, wherein is riot, but be filled with the Spirit; speaking one to another in psalms and hymns and spiritual songs, singing and making melody with your heart to the Lord; giving thanks always for all things in the name of our Lord Jesus Christ to God, even the Father; subjecting yourselves one to another in the fear of Christ.

A word of prayer:

Beloved Lord, we are so thankful that we are in Your presence. We are gathered to You, Lord, and when it comes to the ministry of Your word, You have not left us to our own energy or thoughts, our own talents and gifts, but You have provided us with an anointing so that beyond the human voice we can hear Your voice. And Lord, we do not want to ignore that anointing. We need it, both in the speaking of Your word, in the translating of it, and in the hearing of it. And therefore, Lord, we want to come very simply to say that without You we can do nothing. Nothing will go into eternity unless You are present here by Your Spirit. We want to stand now by faith into that anointing grace and power in full portion for this time, that You will touch our hearts, You will open the eyes of our hearts, You will fill our whole beings with light, and You will meet us in the way that will direct our lives into Your will. And we ask it all in the name of our Messiah, the Lord Jesus. Amen.

It is very interesting that this word, "be ye also ready" in Matthew 24 has this idea of "being equipped," of "being prepared," of "being fitted" for the Lord. I believe that we are going to see tremendous developments within the next years. If we have felt the speed with which things are taking place to be remarkable, the speed with which things will take place in these next years will leave us breathless, because the whole world is deteriorating and there is a sense in which the Lord is withdrawing. That which restrains is being removed, and the mystery of lawlessness is becoming more and more apparent. This lawlessness is not gangsterism, not a mixture of Mafia, Triad, and other sorts of groups along that line. This lawlessness is a deliberate, cold-blooded rejection of the revealed law of God. It is a choice to live apart from the word of God, apart from the law of God. Therefore, there have to be judgments, and there will be greater and greater judgments that we will witness because these things fall upon the righteous and the unrighteous, the saved and the unsaved. Most of us believe in our heads that these days will come at the end of time. Maybe we thought it would not be in our time, and therefore it comes as a bit of a shock to suddenly realize that it is happening all around us. That is why this question of being ready for Christ is all important. In every single sphere we need to be ready for Christ.

I want to talk about what I have called imperatives if we are to be ready for Christ, those things that are absolutely strategic, absolutely essential. It is not something that you can do without. There are a whole lot of things I could talk about in being ready for Christ, but I have selected certain things I believe the Lord wants me to touch upon.

The emphasis of our Lord Jesus is not on the sequence of events. There is a sequence of events, but His emphasis is not on the sequence of events; His emphasis is: "Take heed to yourselves. Be alert. Be watchful. What I say to you, I say to all: 'Watch; be ye also ready, for in an hour you think not the Son of man cometh.'" He is talking to believers. He is talking to the most responsible in the circle of the inner circle—Andrew, Peter, James, and John. And He says to them, "In an hour you think not the Son of man comes."

That has something to say to me as a servant of the Lord who ministers and teaches the word of God. Is it really possible that the Lord will come in an hour that I do not think He is coming? It comes again and again: "In an hour that you think not." So this is a very, very important matter.

Born of God

Now there are some things I am taking for granted that you already know. For instance, you cannot be ready for Christ if you are not born of God, and I do not mean signing a decision card or just sort of putting your hand up. I do not despise that, but I have known many, many people who have done such and were not born of God. They have gotten evangelical phraseology and everything else, but they are not truly converted. They have not been born of the Spirit of God. When a person is born of the Spirit of God, their eyes open, their ears open, and they start to breathe. Before long, they start to walk. Look at yourself. How did you get to where you are now? So many years ago you were just a babe. Someone had to carry you; everything was done for you.

But what happened when you were born? You had eyes, and they opened. My eyes did not open for three weeks. My mother thought I did not have eyes until they finally opened. When they opened, I saw her, and ever since then my eyes have watched and seen things. And my ears opened. I was whacked by the doctor and suddenly I started breathing—and so were you. It is the experience of every one of us.

But if you are going to be ready for the coming of Christ, you must be born again. There is no alternative. It is no good hiding in religion. It is no good hiding in church membership. It is no good hiding in evangelical phraseology. Are you born of God? If you are born of God there will be evidences: "Make your calling and election sure."

Unconfessed Sin

The second thing I am taking for granted is also foundational—unconfessed sin. However much you know the Bible, unconfessed sin renders you totally unready for the coming of the Lord. If there is something in your life that is sin or iniquity—whether it is dishonesty, fraudulence, lying, immorality—and you are hiding it, that thing negates all your Bible knowledge and all your profession. It renders you unready for the coming of the Lord. I take it for granted that if we confess our sin, He is faithful and just to forgive us our sin and to cleanse us from all unrighteousness. Sometimes it costs to confess sin, especially when other people are involved. However, there is no other way to speak about sin than what God says about it. Now those two things I take for granted.

Total Devotion to the Lord Jesus

The first imperative I want to express in being ready for the coming of the Lord when He comes suddenly and unexpectedly is absolute and total devotion to the Person of the Lord Jesus. There is no alternative to total devotion to the Lord Jesus. He is not interested in us working our hands to the bone. He is not interested in us merely trotting around the world preaching the gospel. The first essential imperative is that we are totally devoted to Him. He never said, "Follow the teaching." He never said, "Follow the church." He never said, "Follow Christian leaders." He said, "Follow Me." This imperative finds us out because again and again we get caught up in the rigmarole and routine of Christian living or of church life, and then, somehow or other, in the course of it we lose our first love.

Losing Our First Love
It is interesting that the Lord said right in the beginning, "You shall love the Lord your God with all your soul, with all

your strength, and with all your mind" (see Deuteronomy 6:4). When the Lord Jesus was asked, "What is the greatest commandment?" He said, "Hear O Israel, the Lord our God is one God: and you shall love the Lord your God with all your heart, with all your soul, and with all your mind." And He went on to speak about the second: "You shall love your neighbor as yourself" (see Luke 10:27).

This question of personal devotion to the Lord Jesus is something fundamental to the whole matter of being ready. You cannot be ready if you have lost your love for the Lord Jesus. No amount of Biblical knowledge or Christian work will make up for it. In the final analysis it is a question of your relationship to Him.

For Me to Live is Christ

The apostle Paul gives his testimony in the letter to the Philippians: "For to me to live is Christ and to die is gain" (1:21). We are talking about things being summed up, and here is the apostle's testimony. He said, "Jesus is the sum of my life. For to me to live is Christ, and to die is more of Christ." That is in essence being ready for the coming of the Lord.

In the Colossian letter, Paul says, "When Christ who is our life shall appear, then shall we also appear with Him in glory" (Colossians 3:4). "Christ who is our life..." Isn't that wonderful!

That He Might have the Preeminence

In Colossians 1:18 he says, "And he is the head of the body, the church: who is the beginning, the firstborn from the dead; that in all things he might have the preeminence." It is not that in all things He might have the prominence; it is that in all things He might have the preeminence. The Lord is not interested in being prominent in your life; He is interested in being preeminent in your life. I say this question of being totally devoted to the Person of the Lord Jesus is something tremendous. Why did the Lord say to those apostles: "Follow Me"? Why does He always say to us, "Follow Me"? It has something to do with getting to know Him.

To Fully Know Him

In the letter to the Philippians, 3:10, the apostle gives his testimony again in another way, "That I may know him, and the power of his resurrection, and the fellowship of his sufferings, becoming conformed unto his death."

There is a little prefix in the Greek here that is not so big that we have to translate it but it means, "That I may fully know Him." It is not just "know Him" but "fully know Him." The apostle's whole ministry, his whole work, his service, his life was summed up in this one great passion: to know the Lord. And the more you know the Lord, the more you know that you do not know the Lord. In other words, the more you come to know the Lord, the more you know there is to know of the Lord. It is a vast ocean of experience. This is not just academic knowledge; this is experiential knowledge. You are getting to know the Lord through experience.

Experiential Knowledge

I could give you so many illustrations. I remember once staying with Lady Ogle, and in her drawing room was a little plaque on the wall, and it said, "My peace I give to you." Now I was young, in my twenties, arrogant as only I could be at that age, throwing my weight around telling everybody where they were wrong and sometimes where they were right. And I remember thinking to myself: "What a trite little thing to put up on the wall. There are far more wonderful verses that could have gone up on the wall." But at one point we were talking about battles and troubles which I was in and she was in, and she said, "You see that plaque up there?"

"Yes," I said.

"I was in a terrible, terrible affliction, and I did not know where to turn. Suddenly into my heart came the word: "Peace I leave with you. My peace I give to you." And she said, "In a flash I was different. My situation was the same, but I was different, because I suddenly saw the peace He leaves with us is peace for sins forgiven. He never needed that. That is why He did not call it, 'My peace I leave with you.' It is just, 'Peace I leave with you' because He did not need it. But His peace was the peace He had in Gethsemane when He said, 'Not My will but Yours be done.' And His peace was the peace He had on the cross when He said, 'My God, My God, why have You forsaken Me?' He could say, 'Into Your hands I commend My spirit.' It changed my life."

Now that is experiential knowledge. That is when the word of God leaps out of the Book and becomes flesh and blood. That is when something happens in your life by the word of God that can never be taken away. It is foundational now for the rest of your life. I never forgot that. And when Lady Ogle died, she left that little plaque to me.

I am sure that everyone who has walked with the Lord has had in their own experience times when they did not know what to do or where to turn. Then the Lord breathed a word into the

Imperatives for Being Ready for Christ

situation and that word became theirs. Every time you read it you know something others do not know about that word. It is yours. That is why I find it tremendous that the apostle Peter said in II Peter 3:18: "But grow in the grace and knowledge of our Lord and Savior Jesus Christ." The only way you can grow in the knowledge of the Lord Jesus is by grace. The Lord does not cast pearls before swine. But when you are truly humble and ready to walk with Him, then the Lord reveals and unlocks His secrets. All the treasures of wisdom and knowledge are hidden in the Lord Jesus. And it is so wonderful when you walk with Him and those things become your experience.

Sanctification

This matter of absolute devotion to the Lord Jesus is so tremendous. I think it is basically sanctification. This whole thing about sanctification has become so heavy, so dark, and so religious for some people that it grinds them into the ground. You have to wear black, you have to look miserable, and you cannot do anything; it is like being in a strait jacket. That is not sanctification. The word means "to be set apart." What does it mean to be set apart? Set apart from the world. The Lord has delivered you from the world, delivered you from the power of darkness, and transferred you into the kingdom of His dear Son. But it is not just being in the kingdom; you are set apart to the Lord. You belong to the Lord Jesus. That is sanctification. You are set apart to Him; it is true holiness.

John's Gospel is the most incredible of the four gospels. It is not that I despise the other three. It is just that I think John's Gospel is something unbelievable. It is the most Jewish of the gospels.

I do not think Matthew is as Jewish as everybody says. John is essentially Jewish, and the revelation of the Lord Jesus as the unmentionable name of God, as the I AM, is so tremendous. I AM the Bread of Life. I AM the Door. I AM the Good Shepherd. I AM the Resurrection and the Life. I AM the Way, the Truth, and the Life. I AM the True Vine. It is so wonderful.

When I was first saved, I did not have a Bible, and nobody thought to ask if I possessed one in the wonderful interdenominational Baptist Church I was in which was led by a marvelous Keswick speaker and evangelist, Alan Redpath. They told me to read the Bible but they never gave me one. All I had was a little gospel of John, and I read it and read it and read it until it fell to pieces. This tremendous gospel, which presents the Lord Jesus as God, ends in this way in the last chapter: "Do you love Me?"—three times. In the first two times he uses one Greek word and the last time the other Greek word because Peter could not rise to it. Jesus said, "Do you love Me?" It is not enough to have the theology. It is not enough to have knowledge. It is not enough to be a worker. The question is, "Do you love Me?"

Peter could not rise to it. He said, "Lord, You know I have an affection for You." And the Lord said, "Tend My sheep." He speaks about tending sheep, feeding the lambs, and feeding the sheep. He is not interested in routine Christian work. He is interested in people who are personally devoted to Him, in love with Him, and out of that love comes service. It is the church—the flock, young or old, whatever age we are—whom He asks: "Do you love Me?" Then after He said to Peter, "You will be taken where you would not" (meaning the way he would die), He said, "Follow Me." Isn't that an extraordinary way this tremendous gospel should end? "Do you love me? Then tend My sheep; feed My sheep; feed My lambs; follow Me." How can you and I be ready for the coming of the Lord unless we are in love with the Lord Jesus? Nothing else will satisfy Him and nothing else will make us ready for His coming.

There is no alternative and no substitute for absolute and total devotion to the Person of the Lord Jesus. Knowledge is no substitute; neither is religion or ceremonies or church life, as such, if we make it a thing. In the end, even to an assembly so tremendous as the church in Ephesus, the Lord had to say, "I have this against you. You have left your first love. If you do not repent and return to the first works, then I will remove the lampstand out of its place." That seems incredibility harsh and severe for a company of believers. We could possibly understand it with Laodicea or some of the others. But that gives you an idea of how much the Lord values this matter of personal devotion—knowing the Lord. Do you know the Lord? Do you really know the Lord? Or do you only know Him by what you have read? Do you know Him? Is He someone you actually know? Personal devotion brings us into a personal knowledge of the Lord Jesus.

A Living, Active, Working Faith

The second imperative is a living, active, working faith. Now I am not talking about academic faith. I always remember what James said: "The devil has a kind of faith, and he trembles." At least there is some manifestation. There is no faith other than a living, active, working faith. Faith is not natural. Some people try to say that we all exercise faith when we sit in a chair or we get on a bus or in a plane, as if faith is some natural thing. This is Christian Science faith which teaches that we can pump it up. We sort of expand it or inflate it until we have so much faith we can do something with it such as bulldozing things out of the way. We can get rid of mountains because we have blown up the faith that is in us to do that. Of course, the devil loves this and he comes and whispers these words: "You do not have enough faith. You just do not have enough faith for this problem. You must wait until you get more faith." So you wait and wait and wait; but you will wait until the coming of the Lord. The devil has got you, and he has you right where he wants you. He breathes these words into your ear: "Look at these other people who have such great faith; but you do not have that kind of faith." However, the Lord Jesus said, "If you have faith as a grain of mustard seed you shall say to this mountain, 'Be thou removed;' and it shall be removed." A grain of mustard seed is so small that if I had one seed in the palm of my hand you would not be able to see it. That is how small faith is. All you need is a great Lord and a grain of faith to unite you to the infinity of God, and anything can happen. Nothing is impossible! That is living, active faith.

When the God of glory appeared to our father Abraham and said, "Get out," he went out by faith. He did not analyze himself and say, "Have I got enough faith to get out of here? I must get more faith."—and then try to pump himself up. No, not at all! When he saw the Lord, something happened, and that great aristocrat walked out of that city of Ur to become a shepherd and a cattle herdsman for the rest of his life. It changed him. Such is living, active faith.

I want to underline a verse in this connection because I think it has so much to say to us. Hebrews 11:27 presents it in this way: "By faith Moses forsook Egypt, not fearing the wrath of the king: for he endured, as seeing him who is invisible."

If you and I are going to be ready for the coming of the Lord, we need to endure as seeing Him who is invisible. He cannot be seen with the physical eyes, yet somehow we have to see the invisible One. Now this is a contradiction. How do we see an invisible person? The only way we can possibly see the Lord is outside of reason. That is why I thank God I did not attend a theological seminary because it seems so much like a cemetery to me. So often, seminaries trap you with reason and more reason—everything is reason. Living faith comes from seeing the Lord. Faith, which is the gift of God in us and may be as small as a mustard seed, is activated the moment we see the Lord.

How do we see the Lord since He is invisible? We see with the eyes of our heart. How did Moses see Him who is invisible? It is amazing to us, but He endured. Now there may be a lot to endure in these coming few years, and only those who see Him—who is invisible—will endure. And this has something to do with living, active faith.

Why do you think martyrs are martyrs? How do you think those two great bishops in Britain, in a day when we had godly bishops—Latimer and Ridley—under that dreadful woman Bloody Queen Mary endured? She sentenced them to be burned at the stake. And as they were burning, Latimer said to Ridley: "Play the man, Ridley, for this day we shall set alight a candle that by the grace of God will never go out." (It very well may be going out in Britain.) But how do martyrs go to their death?

If this story I heard about brother Nee is right, he wrote this with his own blood when he was in prison: "I believe that Jesus is my Savior." How could he do that without living faith? How could we do it unless there is living faith, an endurance that comes, not from "Churchillion" grit, but from something God has done in our spirit that enables us to endure to the end?

If we keep our eyes on the Lord Jesus, faith is spontaneously activated. We never get faith by looking in our heart to see how much faith we have. As soon as we do that, the faith we have disappears and literally fades away before our gaze. We get faith by seeing the Lord. Every time we see the Lord, something is spontaneously activated; it is the gift of God.

There are two stories of storms in the gospel of Matthew. One is in chapter 8 where we are told that the Lord got into the boat with His disciples. Of course, the normal way that Christians try to explain it is that He was human, and He was so tired and worn out by all the ministry that He went to the back of the boat and fell fast asleep. A huge storm blew up and all of the apostles were bailing water out furiously, but the water came in faster than they could get it out. Finally, they shook Him and said, "Do You not care that we are about to go down?" All He did was stand up and say, "Hush, be still." And the whole thing stopped.

The second story is in Matthew 14. This time He would not get into the boat which I find very interesting. He refused to get into the boat. He said, "I must send the multitudes away." (A good excuse.) Then He said, "I will meet you on the other side." Another storm came up while the disciples were in the boat, and suddenly they saw Him walking towards them on the water.

They said, "It is a ghost."

But Peter said, "I think it is the Lord;" and he called out: "Is it You, Jesus? Is it you?"

And Jesus said, "Yes."

And Peter said, "If it is You, tell me to come."

And Jesus said, "Come."

The amazing thing is that Peter climbed out of the boat and walked on the water. He had never been to Bible School; he had never read a book about the four steps to walk on water or how you can do the impossible. He saw the Lord, he heard the Lord, he obeyed the Lord, and he did the impossible.

Let us take note of this: if we are to be ready for the coming of the Lord, what is the most important experience we need to have? It is not the stopping of the storm. That reveals the majesty of the Lord Jesus, the power of the Lord Jesus, the sovereign authority of the Lord Jesus, which is wonderful. But it does not help us if we lose the boat and find ourselves in a stormy sea. I suspect (now, I will only know when we get to glory if I am right) that the Lord was hoping the boat would go down while He was asleep in the back, and He would then say to them: "Follow Me!" And they would have all walked on the water. But instead they panicked and said, "Master, You must do something immediately!" And of course when we panic, the Lord has to step in and say, "Stop, stop, be still." But what have we learned? The Lord can stop a storm. But there are times—a day of evil, a time of darkness, a time of insolvable problems—when the Lord does not step in. Then what do we do? It is a tremendous lesson that the Lord taught Peter. He did the impossible when he walked on a stormy sea.

If we want to be ready for the coming of the Lord, here is the greatest lesson we can learn: when the boat is gone and the storm is rolling all around us, to step out and walk on the water with the Lord is tremendous!

We all have the idea that for anything to happen we have to have a tremendous amount of faith. No, we do not. We need very little—only a grain of mustard seed which is so small we could blow it away. Nevertheless, that little grain of mustard-seed faith can unite us to the infinity of God, and then nothing is impossible. Such is faith; and it comes from seeing the Lord. When we see the Lord with the eye of the heart, spontaneously the gift of faith, which is of God, is activated and joins us to the Lord; then tremendous things happen.

A Hearing Ear

A third imperative is a hearing ear. If we want to be ready for the coming of the Lord, we need a hearing ear. The vast numbers of Christians never hear the Lord. I remember years ago brother Sparks quoted to me the Scripture in Romans 8:14: "For as many as are led by the Spirit of God, these are sons of God." And he said to me, "Do you know, Lance, I can count on the fingers of one hand those who are with me in the work who hear the Lord." I was shocked when he said this. I thought to myself: Brother Sparks is a bit too critical. But as I have gotten older I have come to the conclusion that he is right. Many people talk about being led of the Spirit; many people say they are led of the Spirit, but very few people are truly led of the Spirit.

What is a hearing ear? Spiritually, you have within your spirit an organ that can hear the voice of the Lord. It is not extra revelation. Do not get me wrong on this. It is not something that is extra to the Bible—the weird kind of things that get into cultic groups. But when the Spirit of God takes the word of God and makes it alive in us, we are hearing something from the Lord. It is not just words; beyond the words we are hearing the voice of the Lord.

Many people do not believe that they will ever hear the word of the Lord. They think only people like John Wesley, Charles Wesley, Martin Luther, Zwingli, John Calvin or Watchman Nee hear the Lord. The Lord is far too busy to speak to us ordinary mortals. We cannot have a claim on Him like that because He is too busy. We sort of imagine some vast heavenly telephone system with all these voices coming in and the Lord saying, "Yes, yes," and, "yes, yes." So we think we cannot bother Him. But Jesus put it very simply: "My sheep hear My voice." Could there be anything simpler? "My sheep hear My voice." It is very simple. That means the Lord is interested in a relationship with us in which we can hear Him.

Why am I making so much of this as an imperative? In the book of Revelation, the last book of the Bible, which is dealing with the last events that are going to take place, we find this: "He that hath an ear, let him hear what the Spirit saith to the churches," (see Revelation 2: 7, 11, 17, 29; 3:3, 13, 22.

In other words, you will not be ready for the coming of the Lord if you do not hear what the Spirit says to the churches. If you do not have an ear tuned to hear the voice of God in His word, you will never have an understanding of the times in which we live. It is imperative that we have an understanding of the times because people say to me just as it is quoted in II Peter:

"People have always believed the Lord is coming, but all things continue as they were from the beginning of the creation" (see 3:4). We have all these crazy nut cases running around, but there are certain things that have happened in our day and generation that have never happened before since the ascension of the Lord Jesus. This means that certain prophetic milestones have been passed. However long this last phase of world history will last, it has begun, and we are watching something speeding up—almost visibly speeding up. There is a deterioration and a breaking up which is an altogether new system of life being set up.

There are people who believe in human conspiracies, and tell us this: "There are Illuminati and Jewish bankers and tycoons who are doing all this." I personally do not go along with all these conspiracy theories; it is nonsense. But I do believe in one conspirator—Satan. And he is the arch conspirator who is organizing a whole world-wide network and coordinating it with one great aim—to frustrate the purpose of God concerning the Lord Jesus. Thank God, the Lord Jesus will come on time. He will not for one single moment be delayed by all these machinations of Satan and the powers of darkness. He will come on time—neither early nor late.

We do not know the hour or the day. People are always writing these things about when the Lord will come. I remember years ago this man wrote a book called: "Eighty-eight Reasons Why the Lord is Coming Back in 1988." It was to be on such and such a date in September 1988. Everywhere I went people would ask me about this little booklet: "What do you think?" I was so surprised at some of the people who asked me the question because I thought they knew their Bibles better. My response to them was: "Come back in

October and ask me again." The extraordinary thing was that the man who wrote the book then wrote, "Eighty-nine Reasons Why the Lord is Coming Back in 1989." It was to be in September such and such a date in 1989." However, the same thing happened as the other date.

We need to hear what the Lord is saying, and then He gives us an understanding of the times in which we are living. But more than that, we can know what the will of the Lord is. "Be not foolish but understand what the will of the Lord is. Be not unwise but wise, redeeming the time because the days are evil" (see Ephesians 5:15-17). If we hear the Lord we will be redeeming the time. If we hear the Lord, we shall be walking with Him, and we shall be kept within the will of God.

In the Old Testament we have that amazing picture of the leper—the sinner—saved by the grace of God. The priest put the blood first on the ear, then on the thumb, and on the big toe. Most of us would say, "No, no, put the blood on the thumb first. We must do things for the Lord." Others would say, "No, put it on the big toe first. We must walk in the ways of the Lord and fulfill His purpose." But God says, "It is the ear I want. If I do not have the ear, I have neither the hand nor the foot." And then the priest took oil and put it on the ear, on the thumb and on the big toe, as if the Lord is saying, "You not only need a saved hearing, you need a Holy Spirit enlightened hearing." There is no other way.

What a wonderful thing it is when the bondslave says, "I love, I love my master; I will not go out free." The law says, "The master shall take him to the gate and put an awl through his ear." He did not leave him pinned to the gate, but he pierced his ear and put a ring in it. That is not in the Bible, but that is in the Talmud. Then everybody can say, "Look, see that man, he has a ring in his ear. He is a bondslave forever."

Why is the ear so important? Why not put a beautiful ring on his hand with the master's emblem on it? "Let me look at that hand; you belong to such and such a master, and to such a home." Why not put a bracelet on his ankle? Then they would say, "That is some bondslave! He is a fine fellow; he belongs to his master forever." But the Lord has said, "If I do not have his ear, I neither have his hands nor his feet." That is why if you and I want to be ready for the coming of the Lord, it is essential that we have a hearing ear.

Do you know what I consider to be the saddest, most moving, and most plaintive word of our Lord Jesus in the New Testament? It is in Revelation 3:20: "Behold, I stand at the door and knock: if any man hear my voice and open the door, I will come in to him, and will sup with him, and he with me." I find that one of the most moving, plaintive, sad words the Lord has ever spoken. To think He is outside His own church! These are born again believers, evangelicals. They believe, they sing wonderful hymns, they study His word, they have prayer meetings, they have evangelistic times, and the Head of the church, the Savior of the body is outside knocking and saying, "Listen, if any man hear My voice."

If you were to interview those people in that church at Laodicea and say to them: "Listen, the Lord does not think you are hearing Him;" and they would have said, "That is absurd! What a ridiculous suggestion! We love Him. We have His Table. We remember Him. We sing hymns. We study His word. We go out with the gospel

Imperatives for Being Ready for Christ

into the streets. Yes, we are quite wealthy, thank God; and it is the Lord who has given us such wealth." But the Lord was outside. Do you think it is possible for the Lord to be shut outside of an assembly? He did not say, "If you all hear My voice ..." No, He said, "If any man hear My voice ..." It is almost as if He said, "There is no way this church can hear My voice corporately. They are so caught up in their own routine or agenda there is no way they can hear Me." But if there is any man or woman who hears My voice and opens the door, I will come in and sup with him and he with Me."

I can think of nothing more important than to have a hearing ear. So few Christians hear the Lord, and some of those who say they do hear the Lord are crazy. I have to be honest. I have been many, many years among the people of God and there are those who tell me, "The Lord said this and the Lord said that." The Lord has never said anything of the kind, and it is proved by the way things happen in their circumstances and situations that the Lord never spoke to them about these things.

However, I do thank God for those I have known in my life who have truly heard the Lord, and they were quite remarkable people. I remember those two missionaries that spent nearly their whole life on the border of Nepal waiting to go in. When they were first saved, God called them to Nepal and said He would use them to establish the church in Nepal. Dr. Lily O'Hanlon and Lucy Steele lived their lives on the border of Nepal until that day, I shall never forget, when the cable came. I was part of a little prayer meeting and the young people thought I was nuts, praying with all those white haired people. I would pray with them for Nepal once a week, and I was there when the cable came. I have never forgotten it. I felt so big and important, that I had been part of winning a battle to get into Nepal. The cable said, "Tomorrow we go into Nepal. We have been granted permission by the king of Nepal." Out of that came all the work of the Lord in Nepal.

I think of another wonderful old sister who at eighteen years of age was told by the Lord, "You shall serve Me in Afghanistan." She spent her whole life on the border of Afghanistan in what is now Pakistan, and then she had to retire. She did not want to retire but the mission had a retirement policy, and they retired her. Her response was: "All right, I will move into a little home and continue my prayer ministry."

At eighty-two years of age there was a knock on the door and there was a herald from Kabul: "Are you Miss Christenson?"

"I am."

"Are you an eye-specialist nurse?"

"I am."

"The king wants you to come and care for the crown prince who has a serious eye problem."

And that extraordinary lady, when most of us think we are about to toddle into the grave, went into Afghanistan. Through her came Dr. Wilke. And a whole company of Afghanis came to the Lord, most of whom were martyred later by the Taliban. But what a wonderful thing it is to really hear the Lord. A hearing ear is essential if we are going to be ready for the coming of the Lord.

Priorities

Another imperative is priorities. Listen to the word of the Lord Jesus in Matthew's Gospel 6:33: "But seek ye first the kingdom of God, and his righteousness; and all these things shall be added unto you." What a wonderful word! No one can be ready for the coming of the Lord unless he has his priorities right. What do we mean? The context of this word is all to do with eating, clothing, drinking and all the things that make up life—the cares, the worries, and the drudgery of this life. And Jesus said, "Seek ye first the kingdom of God and His righteousness."

He did not excuse any believer—whether it is the housewife, the mother of little children, the husband, the businessman, or the big executive. No one is excused. He said, "Seek ye first the kingdom of God and His righteousness, and all these things shall be added to you."

It has been my experience that the Lord adds and adds and adds once you seek first the kingdom of God and his righteousness. The Lord is so generous and floods us with all things which we need in this life. That is my experience. If we really seek first the kingdom of God and his righteousness, we will not want. Why is this so? We will never go to heaven and say, "Lord, You are in my debt. I did a lot for You, Lord. I worked my hands to the bone for You. I did this and that and so many things, and I am glad to get here now for a bit of rest." I do not think the Lord will ever be in any person's debt. He makes absolutely sure that you and I are in His debt up to the eyeballs. "Seek ye first the kingdom of God and His righteousness, and all these things shall be added to you."

The shortest verse in the New Testament is found in Luke 17:32 within the Lord's word about His return: "Remember Lot's wife." Like a gun going off in the middle of all this teaching about the Lord and His coming, He said, "Remember Lot's wife." Why does He want us to remember Lot's wife? Indeed, she was an amazing woman. She had such a beautiful home and gift of hospitality.

Why did He say, "Remember Lot's wife"? You will recall that the angels had to carry them out because they were so loath to go. As they went out, poor Lot's wife looked back to that lovely home of hers and saw it burning in the fire. The house and everything that belonged to her was ruined. In that moment she was turned to a pillar of salt as a memorial for all believers: "Remember Lot's wife."

In the moment of judgment, turmoil, and colossal tribulation, she looked back. Why did she do that? Her heart was in her home. Some of you would probably say to me: "That is quite mean and hard." Don't judge the Lord. Some people say to me that when the Lord struck Uzzah dead because he steadied the ark, it was a terrible thing to do, but how many times had the Spirit of God wrestled with that arrogant young man? It is the same with Ananias and Sapphira when they fell dead. What a meeting! First, Ananias got up and gave testimony and fell dead. They carried him out and then the wife came in and said the same thing and she fell dead. If we had meetings like that, the fear of God might come upon us all. Someone has said that if the Lord judged everybody the way He judged Ananias and Sapphira, about forty per cent of the church would be dead. And that is probably true.

Let us consider the point in this. I believe that the Lord tried many times to encourage Lot's wife to get her priorities right but she never listened to Him. Her priority was her home and her possessions.

I remember years ago sitting in one of the more guest-house type hotels in Israel in Zohar on the Dead Sea. The whole place was filled with Jewish people. Tourists don't go to that type of hotel, and I was with one of the boys there, sharing a table with a husband and wife. And she looked for a few moments at me and said, "You are Jewish, aren't you?"

And I said, "Yes."

She said, "But your friend here is not."

I said, "No, he isn't."

And in talking to her I could tell from her accent that she was not native born, and I said to her, "Where were you born?"

"Oh," she said, "I was born in Krakow and my husband was born in Lodz."

I said, "How did you survive?"

Her husband said to me: "It is an amazing story. I owned three factories with my brothers. I came home one day and my wife said to me, 'We have got to get out.' I thought, 'Is she mentally unwell? What does she mean?'"

She said, "We have to get out." And then she said, "A strange thought came to me. I could not rest, and I wondered if I was going mad."

Then he went on and said, "She was so upset that I told her to pack a bag and we would get on the train." Immediately he phoned his brothers and said, "Can I leave the factories to you? We are just going away. Something is wrong with my wife and the best thing is to humor her." They went to Kiev in the Ukraine, and very early that next morning the Nazis rolled into Poland. Every member of that family died—one hundred and seventy people. The only ones who survived were her and her husband.

The extraordinary thing was that a year later in Kiev her husband came home and again she said, "We have to go." This time he never questioned it. That same night they got on the Trans-

Siberian Railway and went all the way across to Vladivostok. And the Nazis swept into the Ukraine, and hundreds of thousands were massacred at Babi Yar. That taught me a very simple lesson. How could someone walk out of their home without anything—just shut the door and walk out? "Remember Lot's wife."

On another occasion one of my friends was involved in a fatal accident. I got a phone call from the police to come and help him because he was in such a bad state. So I went to sit with him. After I had been there for awhile, they arranged for him to go back to Norway to appear in a court case. The chief accident officer for Israel took me back in a rental car. On the way, he told me how sorry he was that this had happened to this man who was such a fine fellow. Then I inquired of him: "Where were you born?"

"Berlin," he replied.

"How did you survive?"

And he said, "Oh, there is a story. I was a small boy at the time this happened, and one day when I came out from school, my mother was waiting for me. And she said, 'Now son, I want no argument or questioning, but you are going on a long journey.' We went to the big station in Berlin and my father was there with my sister and my aunt, and we had four little cases. We all got on the Orient Express and went to Turkey. We were smuggled into what was called Palestine then, and we were saved. But every member of our family died."

Then I said, "Do you mean that your mother and father walked out of a beautiful home?" (They were quite wealthy people.)

"Yes," he said, "and we only took small bags with things for sleeping and washing. But the most amazing thing about this whole thing was my aunt. After we became British citizens in

1938 under the mandated territory of Palestine, she said to us: 'I think I will go back to Berlin and settle the property we had there because even though we are not wealthy people anymore, we should get something.' There was a rehabilitation center set up by the Nazis which was actually a façade. She and a friend went back to make a claim. She was taken in, but they would not let the friend in and told her to wait outside. My aunt went through a door and was never seen again."

"Remember Lot's wife." What is this saying to us? We need to get our priorities right. If we are wedded to things—possessions, property, money, all kinds of things—in the moment of turmoil and panic that comes with great upheavals, we will lose everything. We need to keep our eye upon the Lord. We have time now to sort out our priorities. If we are seeking first the kingdom of God and His righteousness, then we do not have to worry about clothing, food or finance.

I have been living dependent upon the Lord since I was seventeen, and I have never for one single moment suffered from not having clothing, food, a home, or much else. The Lord is so incredibly generous. If we seek first the kingdom of God and His righteousness, we do not have to go around living by faith with hints.

I was once in Sweden staying with this family who said to me, "Will you help my son? He is in such a difficult mood."

And I said, "What do you want me to do with your son?"

"Bring him to the Lord," they said. (These two were servants of the Lord, a pastor and his wife.)

My reply to them was this: "I do not do that. First of all, you took the boy out of his bed and put me in his bed, so that makes him an enemy right from the start. Then you expect me to talk to him about the gospel. That is not my business. If he asks me I will certainly speak with him."

One day while I was there, the son said to me, "Excuse me, do you mind me asking you a very straight personal question?"

"No, I do not mind."

He said, "You seem to dress quite nicely. Do you live by faith?"

"Yes, I do," I said. "I live completely dependent upon the Lord. I have never known the Lord to let me down."

"Ah," he said, "you should know my parents."

"Really," I said.

"Yes," he said, "they live by faith, but my mother keeps on saying to my father, 'You must get those holes in the soles of your shoes seen to.' And he said, 'Oh no, because when I kneel in front of the congregation, they see the need to help us.'"

Living by faith with hints does not work. It is much better to live totally dependent upon the Lord. Never tell anyone of your needs. Trust the Lord. I have never found Him to fail. When you get your priorities clear, you are ready for the coming of the Lord. The Lord will take personal responsibility for you, even if you become a martyr. At that moment power will be given to you and grace to go through. You will triumph even in martyrdom.

These are imperatives. We have time now to sort our priorities to make sure that we are seeking first the kingdom of God and His righteousness, and then all these other things will be added in His time and His way. May the Lord make this real for every one of us.

We shall see more and more clearly in the coming years that this world is not worth living in. If you have never longed for the coming of the Lord, you will begin to long for it in a way you have never longed for it before. We are at a tremendous point in history—the deterioration of our society, the return to paganism, the rejection of the Law of God and the word of God (which made the Western nations so great and produced so much civilization, so-called), the spirit of lawlessness, the mystery of lawlessness.

What is the mystery of lawlessness? It is simply that Satan is the conspirator. He is the coordinator and the master mind. It is not human; it is not to do with human philosophies, human ideologies, political parties, educational systems. Behind it all is this arch enemy of our Lord Jesus. And in the end he will be personified in a human being—the antichrist. The spirit of antichrist has been in this world from the very beginning, but in the last phase of world history in which we are now found, it will be personified in a person. He is not a horned individual, but someone very attractive and seemingly democratic—a mixture of autocracy and democracy or iron and clay—two things that do not go together.

The fact of the matter is that the Lord is coming. No man knows the day or the hour, not even the Son nor the angels; only the Father. There is going to come a point in time, somewhere in the not too distant future when the Father says, "Let it roll," and the end will come. It will be simply amazing, just to see the Lord in the clouds of heaven with power and great glory. It is exciting to think about it, and whether we are alive or we have died, we will all be there. We think the people who have died are going to miss out somehow. No, no; they are going to be raised first, and then we which are alive and remain will be caught up together with them. That is something tremendous.

The Great Commission

The fifth imperative is to be involved in the great commission of our Lord Jesus. I have no time for people who are not involved in the commission of the Lord Jesus that cannot be contradicted and cannot be annulled. "Go and make disciples of all nations, and lo, I am with you always even to the end of the age." If we are going to live in little holy huddles without any concern for the unsaved people around us, no concern whatsoever for the dying multitudes in our nation, do you really think we are ready for the coming of the Lord? You cannot make Biblical theology, Biblical doctrine, even the knowledge of the church an excuse for not being involved in this commission of the Lord Jesus.

These words of Jesus are recorded in Matthew 28:18: "All authority and power hath been committed into My hands. Go ye therefore." It is to do with His authority and power at the right hand of God. "Go ye therefore and make disciples of all nations (not converts but disciples), teaching them all things that I have commanded you, baptizing them in the name of the Father and the Son and of the Holy Spirit. And lo, I am with you always, all the way to the end of the age." Do you want the Lord to be with you in the last phase of world history? Then get involved in this great commission of our Lord Jesus.

Mark's Gospel puts it even more simply: "Go into all the world, and preach the gospel to the whole creation" (Mark 16:15). You do not stay and say, "Come." You go. It is the commission of the risen Head of the church.

Please understand me in this. I am not trying to get at anyone, but I have such a burden for this commission to go forth.

Imperatives for Being Ready for Christ

I have noticed everywhere I go in the world that where people have a tremendous burden for the unsaved, the church almost spontaneously begins to develop and grow in their midst. But where there is no burden for the lost and no burden for this dying world, you can spend your whole time talking about deeper things and get nowhere. I speak from a little bit of experience. All over Britain years ago there were these little holy huddle groups I call them, and basically, they were all gathered on deeper teaching. They were faithful, truly born again people. They knew their Bibles inside out and upside down. They really had a knowledge of the Bible, but there was never anybody who ever got saved among them. I am not sure that anyone from the world would have ever felt at home in the group. It was the bane of Mr. Sparks' ministry, and many times he said to me, "This is a curse."

When God begins to work and people truly have a heart for the lost and dying, it is so tremendous. Take note of this—that we cannot be ready for the coming of the Lord if we are not involved in His great commission. Now that does not mean that every one of us becomes an evangelist, nor does it mean that every one of us goes out as a missionary, nor does it mean that we suddenly must get involved in some kind of evangelistic endeavor. What it does mean is that every one of us must have a burden, and out of that will come the church. May God burn this into our spirits.

A Living Sacrifice

"I beseech you therefore, brethren, by the mercies of God, to present your bodies a living sacrifice, holy, acceptable to God, which is your spiritually intelligent worship. And be not fashioned according to this world: but be ye transformed by the renewing of your mind, that ye may prove what is the good and acceptable and perfect will of God. For I say, through the grace that was given me, to every man that is among you, not to think of himself more highly than he ought to think; but so to think as to think soberly, according as God hath dealt to each man a measure of faith. For even as we have many members in one body, and all the members have not the same office: so we, who are many, are one body in Christ, and severally members one of another" (Romans 12:1–5).

The sixth imperative is that we need to be a living sacrifice—not a dead one but a living sacrifice. How amazing it is to me that the apostle Paul summed up the greatest exposition of the gospel and the good news in the Bible in the Roman letter. He had gone through eight chapters speaking of these glad tidings, and it is just tremendous. Then he comes to three chapters which many theologians and Bible teachers say is a kind of parenthesis, and that it was the brilliant mind or genius of the apostle Paul, and he wandered away from what he was teaching. You do not have to worry your little head about it." Others say that it is predestination that he deals with. I say that he deals with the whole question of Israel when he says, "Is it possible to choose and unchoose, to elect and unelect? And if it is possible, what about the church? What about those who have been saved amongst the Gentiles? Will not the same thing happen to them as to the Jews?" Paul deals with this whole thing in three tremendous chapters, and in the end it comes to this incredible word: "I would not, brethren, have you ignorant unto this mystery, lest you be wise in your own conceits, but a hardening in part has befallen Israel, until the full number of the Gentiles be come in; and so all Israel shall be saved, even as it is written: 'There shall come out of Zion the Deliverer.'"

The Scripture, by the way, is that a Redeemer shall come to Zion, and that was fulfilled. But the Septuagint and the ancient Greek version of the Old Testament does not say this. We do not know where Paul got it from, but he said, "As it is said, there shall come out of Zion the Deliverer, he shall turn away ungodliness from Jacob." The original in the Hebrew in Isaiah 59 is this: "A Redeemer will come to Zion, and to those that turn away from ungodliness in Jacob" (see v. 20). And that is exactly what happened in the early church. But in this amazing prophetic statement he says, "There shall come out of Zion the Deliverer; he shall turn away ungodliness from Jacob: And this is my covenant unto them, when I shall take away their sins. As touching the gospel, they (the Jewish people) are enemies for your sake: but as touching the election, they are beloved for the fathers' sake. For the gifts and the calling of God are irrevocable" (see Romans 11:26b–29).

Let it sink in: the gifts and calling of God are irrevocable. Then he comes to the summing up, not only the first eight chapters but also chapters 9, 10, 11: "I beseech you therefore, brethren, by the mercies (plural) of God, to present your bodies a living sacrifice, holy, acceptable to God, which is your spiritually, intelligent worship" (see Romans 12:1).

So, is a living sacrifice the end of the gospel? Yes. "Oh," you say, "I thought the gospel was that we should be very happy, very joyful, that everything will be done for us. If we have any messes the Lord will clean it all up." No, the end of the gospel is a living sacrifice.

There is real emotion in worship, and there is nothing wrong with it, but there is another kind of worship that is far more important. This Greek construction is so difficult. Some say, "Your rational worship" or "your rational service."

I once spoke with one of the Greek dons of Cambridge about this: "What do you really think it means? If I were to say, 'spiritually, intelligent worship,' is that correct?" He said, "It is absolutely correct. That is what it means."

It is a cold-blooded decision—spiritually intelligent. It is not suddenly as in a moment of emotion. It is not in a meeting in the height of emotion that you consecrated yourself but in a deliberate, cold-blooded way you said, "I will be a living sacrifice." There is no alternative nor substitute for this. If you and I are to be ready for the coming of the Lord, we need to be a living sacrifice—whether we are young or old people. I thank God, with all my faults and failings I was only fourteen or fifteen years of age when I chose to be a living sacrifice. Young people, do not think this is for the older ones; this is for everyone. It is the gateway into so much in our spiritual life.

Personal Life

"And be not fashioned according to this age." The word is "molded." Be not conformed—be not in a strait jacket of this age. Most of us are influenced. Look at the way we dress and the fashions we have. We are all influenced by the generation in which we live or the age in which we live. We cannot help it. The only way out of being molded or fashioned according to this age is by being a living sacrifice. That is the time you have settled it, and you are out. You are free as a bird out of a cage. Otherwise, you always have this problem of a Christian self-life. You say, "No, no, no, what do you mean?" I mean this. The problem is a converted self-life. It is all self—I, I, I, me, me, me. What am I getting out of this conference? What am I getting out of the Lord? What am I getting out of this ministry? What am I getting out of life? It is always I. This self-life is the curse of the church—rivalry, jealousy, ambition, competition, gossip, back-biting. It is all within every one of us. The sweetest people become almost demonic when put into the right conditions. Believe me, I have met them. They seem so sweet, so modest, so humble, until they are put into conditions in which somehow or other the real self within them comes out into the open. How can you get that self-life dealt with? It is only by being a living sacrifice.

Service and Church Life

It is not only your personal life that needs dealing with; it is also your service. If the self-life is the basis and energy of your Christian service, it will be destroyed and it will destroy others. It is the same with church life. If it is a collection of self-lives, all trying to be together, it will be a cacophony, if you understand what I mean—one great noise from all these self-lives claiming some kind of place amongst us.

We in Christian circles have made a tremendous mistake. I always get people upset with me over saying this, but I am going to say it. Excuse me for being so arrogant, but I am quite sure I am right on this matter. We will say to people: "Do you have a gift? You have a gift of the gab; you must be a preacher. We must have you. Anyone who has a silver tongue is wonderful. God gave you that."

"Are you an organizer? That is great; consecrate your organizing gift to God." I have known people who have organized the Holy Spirit out of anything they have taken up. I have seen it with my own eyes and experienced it. They are so clever in organizing; they can do it from coast to coast and from continent to continent; the greater the organizer, the greater the problem. Brother Nee once said, "We suffer more from the talents and the gifts of the members of the body than we do from their failings and sins."

"Are you clever at music? Consecrate it to the Lord. Have you got a voice to sing? Offer it to the Lord." But we all know what happens when we hear someone singing and all we are left with is their singing. Oh, wonderful; what a lovely voice. Another person sings and we are in the presence of the Lord. One person plays an instrument and all you are left with is their instrumental playing. Another person plays and you are worshiping the Lord. One person speaks and ministers (we have to use words), and you hear the Lord. Another person speaks and all you hear is them. All natural gifts have to go to the cross, and it is up to the Lord, after those gifts go through death, burial, and resurrection, whether they will be greatly used of God or whether they are left in the grave.

Renewing Your Mind
"I beseech you therefore, brethren, by the mercies of God to present your bodies a living sacrifice, holy, set apart, acceptable, well pleasing to God which is your spiritually, intelligent worship.

And be not fashioned according to this age, formed according to this age, molded according to this age: but be ye transformed by the renewing of your mind" (see Romans 12:1–2).

The trouble in church life is the mindset of its members. When we become a living sacrifice, the Holy Spirit is able to transform us by the renewing of our mind. There is nothing more wonderful than to see a sinner become a saint. There is nothing more wonderful than to see someone who is small and crabby and mean, somehow in the end, becoming Christ-like. There is nothing more wonderful than to see a selfish person in the end laying down their life and serving others. It is moving.

This same apostle wrote another letter to the Philippians and said, "Have this mind in you which was also in Christ Jesus" (Philippians 2:5). It is much the same thing; it is not the same word in Greek, but it is much the same idea. Have this attitude, or have this mindset. What was this mindset? The Lord Jesus never thought being on an equality with God something to be fought over or grasped at or held on to, but He humbled Himself. He took the form of a bondslave and became obedient even unto death.

What is a living sacrifice? It is all to do with death. When we are prepared to die, God exalts us. I have seen it a thousand times in the arguments, squabbles, and fights that Christians have with one another. When they fight with one another, God says, "I leave you to it. Fight it out." But when one side says, "We will not fight; we will die," God takes their place and the collision course is set. We can talk until we are blue in the face about the kingdom of God, the church, or the eternal purpose of God, but if we cannot forgive another brother or sister, something is wrong. And we know that the Lord has said very simply in the pattern prayer: "If you do not forgive others for their trespasses, neither will My heavenly Father forgive you." That means if we have an unforgiving spirit, our prayers are worthless. That is how serious this matter is.

I think it is brilliant of the Holy Spirit to so work in this way that in one swoop we can settle everything. "Remember Lot's wife?" If she had only been a living sacrifice it would have been entirely different. It changes everything. When you die, God takes over in resurrection. When you let go, God steps in, and He molds and fashions and gives back. When you humble yourself, God lifts you up. "A living sacrifice"—is it any wonder that it is called your spiritually, intelligent worship?

Let me take you a step further. The apostle goes on and says here in this amazing chapter: "For I say, through the grace that was given me, to every man that is among you. not to think of himself more highly than he ought to think; but so to think as to think soberly, according as God hath dealt to each man a measure of faith. For even as we have many members in one body, and all the members have not the same office: so we, who are many, are one body in Christ" (Romans 12:3–5a).

How do we get a functioning church? This is a good question. Some people have been working at having a church for years and years and years, and still it never comes. How can we get a functioning church that actually functions? The only way is when we have a nucleus of people who are living sacrifices, and then God blesses the selfish. You can have babes, and you can have those who have been arrested in their development and become almost a trial to the church, but the church can still function. It comes out of those who are living sacrifices.

Proving the Will of God

"That you may prove what is the good and acceptable and perfect will of God." I say we all have problems with the will of God if we are honest. Some of us, especially younger people are frightened at the will of God—afraid that the Lord may make you a monk or a nun, He might require you not to marry, or He might send you to the ends of the earth and you do not want to go. So of course you are frightened at the will of God because that self-life of yours is intact. It is a converted self-life, and it is being beautifully dolled up and Christianized. When we become living sacrifices, we will prove the good, acceptable, and perfect will of God. Sometimes the will of God is difficult. Sometimes it leads you through the valley of the shadow of death. Sometimes it leads through difficult times, desert times, even times of famine, but it is always good, acceptable, and perfect. Nevertheless, when we come out the other end, we give glory to God. We would not have it any other way.

If you and I truly want to see what the church is, we are going to have to become living sacrifices. We all need to ask ourselves: "Am I a living sacrifice?" I used to be so frightened of the wonderful old hymn written by a Scots divine, George Matheson: "O Love That Wilt Not Let Me Go." I thought the last verse was so terrifying:

> *O Cross, that liftest up my head,*
> *I dare not ask to fly from Thee;*
> *I lay in dust life's glory dead;*
> *And from the ground there blossoms red,*
> *Life that shall endless be.*

He was going blind, and the specialist explained to him: "You will be totally blind for the rest of your life." He was a young man, only in his twenties, pastor of the Church of Scotland, near where Mr. Sparks was born. And his fiancée dumped him the moment she heard what the specialist said, and he wrote this amazing hymn: "O Love That Wilt Not Let Me Go." But I always found that last verse terrifying. I knew that you could not ask to fly from the cross; but to lay in dust with life's glory dead is a position of faith. It is impossible to do it unless the Spirit of God is in you. We cannot be ready for Christ if we are not a living sacrifice. It is as simple as that.

Indwelt, Filled, and Anointed with the Holy Spirit

The seventh imperative is to be indwelt, filled, and anointed with the Holy Spirit. There is no way for any child of God to be ready for the coming of the Lord if they are not indwelt, filled, and anointed with the Holy Spirit. On this matter there is a lot of confusion, but the word of God is simple. Forget the confusion, and face the word of God: "Be filled with the Holy Spirit."

Some people say to me, "Yes, of course, we are all filled with the Holy Spirit." Really? Well, that is a big surprise to me. I have been amongst Christians for years and years, and I can tell you those who are filled with the Holy Spirit and those who are not.

Some people say, "It is a question of faith; we are not really expecting to feel anything." But everybody else can see whether we are filled with the Holy Spirit because it is obvious. How in the world did the apostles say to them: "Choose you out men who are filled with the Holy Spirit," unless it is possible to see that they are filled with the Holy Spirit? It is true that the Holy Spirit can dwell in us bottled up and in a strait jacket, and closed within our flesh.

I find it tremendous that John the Baptist described the ministry of the Lord Jesus as He that baptizes in the Spirit and fire (see Matthew 3:11). I cannot accept any explanation of this that is less than something wonderful. John the Baptist said, "I baptize in water unto repentance." That was the heart of his ministry. "But He that comes after me will baptize in the Spirit." In the Greek it can say either "in the Spirit" or "with the Spirit" or "by the Spirit." I prefer "baptized in the Spirit" because in water baptism it is being pushed under the water. I do not believe in sprinkling or a little bit of water in a cross on a head. We know that is not how we bury a person. We put them down in the ground and the soil goes over them. Therefore it is a proper baptism when you go under the water.

The baptism of the Spirit surely must be a term that is inclusive of the whole ministry of the Holy Spirit—the birth by the Holy Spirit, the indwelling of the Holy Spirit, the being filled with the Holy Spirit, the fruit of the Spirit, and the anointing of the Spirit.

When you are young in the Lord, you say, "The Holy Spirit is in me; He is indwelling me." That is correct, the Holy Spirit is in you; you do have the Holy Spirit. But the baptism of the Spirit is when the Holy Spirit gets you. There is a vast difference between you having the Holy Spirit and the Holy Spirit having you.

Who is it that baptizes you? It is the Lord Jesus, not the Spirit. I know there is a great deal of discussion about this, and I personally also believe that Pentecost is historic. It is once and for all. When the Lord Jesus sat down at the right hand of God, He received the promise of the Holy Spirit and poured forth this which you see and hear. But in that pouring out of the Holy Spirit two or three things happened at once—the indwelling of the Holy Spirit, being born of the Spirit, being filled with the Spirit, and being anointed with the Spirit. That is how I see it. And I have an argument with people who tell me, "It is historic." Of course it is historic; so is Calvary. I came to the Lord in 1943, but Jesus was crucified some one thousand, nine hundred years ago. However, when I believed on the Lord Jesus, in that moment, the historic event of Calvary became mine, and I was born of God. I became a child of God, saved by the grace of God through the atoning work of my Messiah Jesus. Likewise, so did you.

I used to hear about the Holy Spirit, but it was four or five years later before I experienced the Holy Spirit. I was still a youngster in my teens, but I was so tired of the Christian life with its legalism and routines. I read my portion of the Scriptures every day, I said my prayers every day, and I tried to witness to one person every day. I did all these things, and the whole thing was law after law after law, and no joy. Neither did it help me to see Christians who obviously were in the same condition as myself.

And then, one day, a little book came into my hands. I decided to spend the whole afternoon on my knees in a dusty old Church of England behind the school of Oriental and African Studies in the University of London reading this book. It was as if heaven opened, and the first thing that came to me was this: the Holy Spirit is the Vice-Regent of Christ and is here to produce His nature and character and life in me. It was such a shock to me. I said to the Holy Spirit: "I never knew You were a Person; therefore, I never addressed You before." And by the way, I do not think it is necessary to address the Holy Spirit because we pray to the Father by the Spirit in the name of Jesus. But nevertheless, I said, "Dear Holy Spirit, I am so sorry; I have totally ignored You. Here are the keys of my life. Do exactly what You want to do in me."

That was the beginning of my living the Christian life and of my ministry. It was not over. Then it was as if the Lord opened something more in heaven and I understood I was crucified with Christ. Oh, what a fight it was. Me, crucified with Christ? I had been trying to make myself to be such a good Christian. "Yes," the Lord said, "my estimate of you is to have you crucified with My Son." Oh, that was such a shock! There I was trying to get the old Lance to pray, to use evangelical phraseology, Biblical phraseology, sing wonderful hymns, try to look cheerful, try to win somebody else to the Lord. I never, ever got anywhere near any of it. And then in some wonderful way I understood that I had been crucified with Christ. I can honestly say that a huge load rolled off my back. For the first time in years, I laughed. That was the burden the Christian life had been to me. It just rolled off, and I thanked God.

Some people say you must have the cross first and then an experience of the Holy Spirit. This may be some people's experience but mine was that the Holy Spirit came first and then the cross. I could not put to death the deeds of the body without the Holy Spirit. I could not fall into the ground and die without the Holy Spirit. I could not become a living sacrifice apart from the Holy Spirit. It was the Holy Spirit who empowered me to do it, and in that afternoon when I somehow met the Lord, my calling was confirmed and the ministry God gave me became mine. I actually went out but not to do anything. The Lord said to me, "No more witnessing." Oh, how thankful I was. "No more witnessing," the Lord said, "not until I give you the opportunity." For three weeks I lived a carefree life. For the first time, I smiled and enjoyed myself. In the old days every time I went to the commons room, the other students moved away because they knew I would be onto them about being saved or converted or coming to a meeting. When I went down a corridor, I do not know how many of them got in the wrong lectures because they vanished into any door to get out of the way.

I was sitting in the students' commons room when the fellow who was the captain of the rugby team came up and said, "Do you mind me asking you a personal question or two?"

"No," I said.

"We have been talking and we see something different about you. What is it?"

Of course, a few weeks earlier I would have said to him, "You are a sinner, and I am saved by the grace of God. I am going to glory and you are going to hell." That was my way of evangelizing. But instead I looked at him and then I said, "Well, we are both sinners, but by the grace of God I have been saved by the Lord Jesus. Maybe you have not had such an experience."

And he looked at me and said, "How can I have such an experience?" And a tear began to run down his face, and I was convinced that it must be the devil because I had tried to get people saved for three years and no one ever got saved. Here was this great big hulk of a man with a tear running down his cheek saying to me, "How can it happen to me? Do I have to go to a church and kneel in the church?"

"No," I said.

He said, "Do I have to go somewhere special, to some private room?"

"No," I said.

"Well then, here?"

Without thinking I said, "Of course, anywhere."

And with that he suddenly just said, "Oh God, You know what a sinner I am. Come into my heart and save me."

And then I thought to myself: this cannot be the Lord. How could it happen so easily? Here I am laboring and laboring and laboring, and suddenly this man bursts into tears. It was the beginning of a whole number of others who came to the Lord.

Don't be afraid of the Holy Spirit. Don't grieve the Holy Spirit. Don't quench the Holy Spirit. The Holy Spirit is here to glorify the Lord Jesus. He is here to take us and make us what the Lord Jesus wants us to be. It is a wonderful thing to be led of the Spirit of God. It is a wonderful thing to be a temple of the Holy Spirit. It is a wonderful thing to be immersed in the greatness of the Holy Spirit because He never talks about Himself nor draws attention to Himself. He is always turning our gaze upon the Lord Jesus and enabling us to praise and glorify Him.

How can we be ready for the coming of the Lord—equipped, fitted out, and prepared—but by the Spirit of God? How are we going to stand in these days of turmoil and deterioration and break-up unless we have the power of the Holy Spirit? Don't be afraid of these words: "the power of the Holy Spirit." Even our Lord Jesus, who was born of the Spirit and filled with the Spirit, was thirty years of age when He was anointed of the Holy Spirit to die daily until He came to Calvary and went through that death on the cross. It was the Holy Spirit who enabled Jesus to offer

Himself up on the cross, and it was the Holy Spirit who raised Him from the dead. Don't be afraid of the Holy Spirit.

Fire

This is the thing that most burdens me. The trouble with most believers is that they cannot bring themselves to say they need to return to the Lord. They think it is sort of letting the side down. It is an embarrassment to say, "Me? Return to the Lord? With all my knowledge?"

The thing that most disturbs me is that there is no fire. "Oh," you say, "are you a Pentecostal?" No, but where there is fire I am always thankful—not strange fire, not foreign fire, not demonic fire—the fire of God. When the fire of God burns in a human being, others are brought to the place where they can see. Have you ever noticed how every time there is a big fire men come and stand there looking? It is a very strange thing about men, but they seem to love fires.

Fire attracts; fire warms, fire is energy; fire is power. It is not for nothing that fire is a symbol of the Holy Spirit. It is not for nothing that when the Holy Spirit was poured out by the Lord Jesus at the right hand of the Father it distributed itself in a flame of fire on every one of the one hundred and twenty. Every one of them was alight and on fire. I find it so sad when I go over the world to assemblies that have great knowledge of the word of God and the purpose of God—and no fire. That is not how it was in the beginning. You and I need the fire of God and we cannot be ready for the coming of the Lord unless we have that fire. May God speak to every one of our hearts.

Being an Overcomer

Finally, the eighth imperative is to be an overcomer. I do not know why people get terribly afraid of the word overcomer. They think it is elitist. Every child of God is meant to be an overcomer. What does it mean to be an overcomer? It simply means "to come over." Whatever the obstacle is, we come over it. Whatever stands against us, we come over it. How can you and I be overcomers? The only way is by the Overcomer in us. Jesus said, "Be of good cheer; I have overcome the world."

When the Lord Jesus, by the Spirit, dwells in us unhindered, unrestricted, we can be nothing else but an overcomer. How I love Margaret Barber's hymn: "Make Me An Overcomer." I wish I could quote all the phrases from that hymn, but here is a little one: "In power within me live…" And here is another one: "Come Lord, bend from the Glory, on me Thy Spirit cast…" She got it. You cannot be an overcomer apart from the Holy Spirit. Of course, you must be a living sacrifice.

They Overcame by the Blood of the Lamb

How beautiful is the little formula we have in Revelation 12-11: "They overcame him by the blood of the Lamb, by the word of their testimony, and they loved not their lives to the death." The only way to be an overcomer is to have a fixation on the finished work of the Lord Jesus. There is no other way. Otherwise the devil will get you. He will fire his fiery darts at you and try to get in through some little chink in the armor. He will get you some way or other unless you know the finished work of the Lord

Jesus. That is the shield of faith, the helmet of salvation, the loins girded with truth, and the feet shod with the gospel of peace.

You will never be an overcomer because you are something in yourself. You will never become an overcomer because you have great knowledge or zeal. You will be an overcomer through the blood of the Lamb. Stand there, withstand, and having done all stand.

Many years ago the young people from Halford House would go up to Mr. Sparks' home in Scotland in the summer. They would have great times, and Mr. Sparks himself became a different person with those young people. I remember on one occasion someone said, "Brother Sparks, what is an overcomer?" He thought for a while and then said, "An overcomer is not someone who is perfect or elite or superman; an overcomer is someone who is in the will of God at the end of their earthly life." They had remained, or if they had gotten out of it somewhere, they had returned to the center of God's will. That is an overcomer. Every time we fail, every time we fall, every time we sin, every time the enemy has ground to come to us and shoot us down—the blood of the Lamb cleanses us.

The Word of Their Testimony

"And the word of their testimony." What a wonderful second phrase this is! What does it mean? It means that with their lips they confess that Jesus is Lord. They articulate, or to use an American phrase, they verbalize their testimony. When ones say: "I hope, I think, maybe," that is no testimony. But when we say, "He is Lord"—that is a testimony. "He is on the throne—that is a testimony. When we say, "He has won the victory"—that is a testimony. When we say, "Truth will win"—that is a testimony. When we say, "The church will be built"—that is the word of testimony. We actually articulate it and speak it out. And through that word of testimony we overcome.

They Loved Not Their Lives unto Death

The third thing is just as amazing. "They loved not their lives even to the death." How do we understand it? Does it mean martyrdom? Maybe. Or does it mean that they were living sacrifices right through to their home going?

We know the Lord is coming. Are we ready? Are we ready for the Lord? How incredibly gracious the Lord is! He is not some severe school master or principal who stands there with enormous severity. He wants to help us. He wants us to be ready. Those were His words: "Therefore be ye also ready, for in an hour that ye think not the Son of Man comes." Can we hasten the coming of the day of God? Is it possible for us in some way through our devotion, through our being made ready, our returning to the Lord, our living in Him and with Him, can we hasten the coming of the day of God? There is some reason why it says, "No one knows the day or hour, not even the angels or the Son." Why is it that the Father waits to give the word? Could it be that our devotion has something to do with it? Is it because of our unreadiness to pay the price to be what He wants us to be? Is it because of the little arguments we have with the Lord, the murmurings, the rebellions, the obstacles that we somehow set in our way? How stupid they are when you think about it! May the Lord touch our hearts and may He, by the Spirit of God, make us ready, set us on fire, bring us back to our first love, fill us and anoint us with the Holy Spirit so that we might become overcomers by His grace alone.

Shall we pray?

Lord, take these poor words and write them indelibly in our hearts. Don't let us get away from this, Lord. Follow us until You get what You want in us. We want to see Your purpose fulfilled. We want to see the bride make herself, by Your grace, ready. We want to see the gospel preached in all the world. We want to see the body of our Lord Jesus built up. We want to see You be not only the beginning but the end for every one of us. Lord, hear us and let Your word dwell in us richly. We ask it in the name of our Lord Jesus. Amen

Other books by Lance Lambert can be found on lancelambert.org

Gathering Together Volume 1

What is the church? What is the basis for meeting together as the church? What is true fellowship? What is the priesthood of all believers? What is the difference between unity and uniformity in the church? In this book, the first volume of Gathering Together, Lance Lambert answers these questions and many more. In doing this, he emphasizes the absolute headship of Christ and the oneness of the body of Christ.

Gathering Together Volume 2

Do you want to see the church in practical expression on earth in our day? Do you want to see the glory of the latter house exceed that of the former? What is the secret, the key to the source of the life of God in which everything lies inherent? The house of God is going to be built; it must be built. The top stone will be brought forth one day with shouts of "Grace, grace to it." Let us seek the Lord that we may see that day!

Talks With Leaders

"O Timothy, guard that which is committed unto thee ..." ~ 1 Timothy 6:20 Has God given you something? Has God deposited something in you? Is there something of Himself which He has given to you to contribute to the people of God? Guard it. Guard that vision which He has given you. Guard that understanding that He has so mercifully granted to you. Guard that experience which He has given that it does not evaporate or drain away or become a cause of pride. Guard that which the Lord has given to you by the Holy Spirit. In these heart-to-heart talks with leaders Lance Lambert covers such topics as the character of God's servants, the way to serve, the importance of anointing, and hearing God's voice. Let us consider together how to remain faithful with what has been entrusted to us.

Till the Day Dawns

And we have the word of prophecy made more sure; whereunto ye do well that ye take heed, as unto a lamp shining in a dark place, until the day dawn, and the day-star arise in your hearts. ~ II Peter 1:9

The word of prophecy was not given that we might merely be comforted but that we would be prepared and made ready. Let us look into the word of God together, searching out the prophecies, that the Day-Star arise in our hearts until the Day dawns.

The Uniqueness of Israel

Woven into the fabric of Jewish existence there is an undeniable uniqueness. Israel's terrain, her history and chief city, all owe their uniqueness to the fact that God's appointed Saviour for the world was born a Jew. His destiny and theirs are forever intertwined.

There is bitter controversy over the subject of Israel, but time itself will establish the truth about this nation's place in God's plan. For Lance Lambert, the Lord Jesus is the key that unlocks Jewish history He is the key not only to their fall, but also to their restoration. For in spite of the fact that they rejected Him, He has not rejected them.

www.ingramcontent.com/pod-product-compliance
Lightning Source LLC
Chambersburg PA
CBHW061338040426
42444CB00011B/2975